THE SIX FIGURE BARBER BLUEPRINT:

The Official How-To-Guide On Building Clientele At A Fast Pace

Dack Douglas

Icon Publications Limited

CONTENTS

Introduction

Welcome to "The Six-Figure Barber Blueprint: The Official How-To-Guide On Building Clientele At A Fast Pace," where the art of grooming meets the science of success. In this transformative guide, we invite you to embark on a journey that will not only sharpen your skills as a barber but also empower you to flourish as a prosperous entrepreneur in the dynamic world of grooming and style.

Barbering is an age-old craft that transcends time and cultures. As barbers, we hold the power to shape not only hair but also the confidence and self-esteem of our clients. We are the trusted confidants, the image-makers, and the architects of personal style. But in today's rapidly evolving landscape, talent alone is no longer enough to ensure lasting success.

The modern barbering industry demands a new breed of professionals—barberpreneurs who blend their artistic mastery with savvy business acumen. To achieve six-figure success, you must embrace the true potential of your craft and unleash the entrepreneur within.

In "The Six-Figure Barber Blueprint," we have gathered the collective wisdom of seasoned barbers and industry experts who have not only honed their skills to perfection but have also unlocked the secrets to building thriving, lucrative careers. We will guide you through every aspect of this transformative journey, leaving no stone unturned in our pursuit of excellence.

From mastering the art of precise fades, intricate designs, and the perfect line-up, to understanding the intricacies of branding, marketing, and financial management, this blueprint is your ultimate companion on the path to triumph. We believe that success is not just about creating stunning haircuts, but also about cultivating meaningful connections with clients and forging a strong personal brand that stands out in a crowded marketplace.

THE 6 FIGURE BARBER BLUEPRINT: THE OFFICIAL HOW-TO-GUIDE ON BUILDING CLIENTELE AT A FAST PACE

CHAPTER 1: INTRODUCTION TO BARBERING

1a. The History And Evolution Of Barbering

Barbering has a rich history that dates back thousands of years. The profession of barbering can be traced back to ancient civilizations, such as Egypt and Greece. In ancient Egypt, barbers not only cut hair but also played a significant role in religious ceremonies and rituals.

During the Middle Ages, barbers were not only responsible for grooming hair but also performed medical procedures like bloodletting and minor surgeries. This dual role as both barber and surgeon led to the iconic symbol of barbers, the barber's pole, which represented bloodied bandages.

As time progressed, the profession of barbering evolved, and barbershops became social hubs where men gathered to chat, exchange news, and discuss local matters. In the 19th century, the popularity of facial hair and beard grooming led to specialized barbershops dedicated to providing services for grooming facial hair.
In the early 20th century, the invention of safety razors and electric clippers transformed the barbering industry, making haircuts and grooming more accessible and efficient.

In recent decades, barbering has experienced a resurgence in popularity with the revival of traditional grooming techniques and styles. Modern barbershops have become trendy and stylish establishments, offering a range of services beyond haircuts, such as beard trims, hot towel shaves, and grooming products.

Today, barbering continues to be an essential part of grooming culture, combining traditional practices with contemporary trends to meet the grooming needs of people worldwide.

1b. Understanding The Modern Barbering Industry

Understanding the modern barbering industry involves a combination of research and hands-on experience. Here are some steps to help you gain insight into the industry:

Research: Start by reading articles, books, and online resources about the history and evolution of barbering. Look for information on current trends, popular styles, and the latest techniques used by modern barbers.

Visit Barbershops: Spend time visiting various barbershops in your area to observe how they operate, interact with customers, and what services they offer. Take note of the ambiance, decor, and the overall experience they provide to their clients.

Talk to Barbers: Engage in conversations with professional barbers to gain firsthand knowledge about their experiences, challenges, and tips for success in the industry. They may provide valuable insights into the day-to-day operations of a barbershop.

Attend Barbering Events and Trade Shows: Look for industry events and trade shows related to barbering. These gatherings often feature demonstrations, workshops, and networking opportunities that can help you understand the latest trends and techniques.

Online Communities and Forums: Join online forums and social media groups dedicated to barbers and the barbering industry. Engaging with others in these communities can provide you with a broader perspective and allow you to ask questions directly to experienced barbers.

Take Barbering Courses: If you're serious about pursuing a career in barbering, consider enrolling in a reputable barbering school or taking online courses. These programs can provide you with formal training and hands-on experience under the guidance of experienced instructors.

Stay Updated: Keep yourself informed about the latest trends, products, and techniques in the barbering industry by following industry-specific publications, blogs, and social media accounts.

Practice and Learn: If possible, practice basic grooming skills on friends or family members to gain some experience. Continuous learning and practice are essential for improving your barbering skills.

Remember that the barbering industry is not just about cutting hair but also about customer service, creating a welcoming environment, and understanding the diverse needs of clients. By combining research with practical experience, you can gain a deeper understanding of the modern barbering industry and its potential opportunities.

1c. The Qualities Of A Successful Barber

Several qualities contribute to the success of a barber. Here are some key traits that successful barbers often possess:

Technical Skill: A successful barber has excellent technical skills in cutting and styling hair, shaping beards, and performing various grooming services. They stay up-to-date with the latest techniques and trends to offer the best services to their clients.

Creativity: Successful barbers demonstrate creativity in creating unique and personalized hairstyles and grooming solutions for their clients. They can suggest suitable styles based on individual preferences, face shapes, and hair types.

Customer Service: Providing exceptional customer service is vital for a successful barber. Good communication, active listening, and a friendly demeanor help build a strong rapport with clients, leading to customer loyalty and positive word-of-mouth.

Attention to Detail: Barbers must pay close attention to detail to achieve precise and polished haircuts and grooming outcomes. Clients appreciate barbers who are meticulous in their work.

Time Management: Managing time efficiently is crucial in a busy barbershop. Successful barbers can balance providing quality services while respecting their clients' schedules.

Professionalism: Being professional in appearance and behavior creates a positive impression on clients. Punctuality, cleanliness, and maintaining a well-organized work area are essential aspects of professionalism.

Adaptability: The barbering industry is ever-evolving, with new trends and techniques emerging regularly. Successful barbers are adaptable and open to learning and incorporating new skills into their practice.

Business Acumen: If a barber plans to run their own barbershop, having basic business knowledge is essential. Understanding financial management, marketing, and customer retention strategies can contribute to the success of the business.

Confidence: Confidence in their skills and abilities allows barbers to approach each client with assurance, helping clients feel comfortable and trust their expertise.

Empathy: Successful barbers show empathy and understanding towards their clients' needs and preferences. They consider clients' input while providing recommendations for suitable styles and grooming services.

Passion: Passion for the art of barbering fuels the drive to excel in the profession. Successful barbers genuinely enjoy their work and take pride in making their clients look and feel their best.

By embodying these qualities, a barber can not only provide excellent services but also build a loyal clientele and establish a successful and rewarding career in the industry.

* * *

CHAPTER 2: GETTING STARTED IN BARBERING

2a. Choosing The Right Barbering School Or Apprenticeship

Choosing the right barbering school or apprenticeship is essential for laying a strong foundation for your career as a barber. Here are some steps to help you make the best decision:

Research Schools and Programs: Start by researching different barbering schools and apprenticeship programs in your area or places you're willing to relocate to. Look for programs that have a good reputation and are recognized by industry professionals.

Check Accreditation: Ensure that the school or apprenticeship program you consider is accredited or affiliated with relevant barbering associations or governing bodies. Accredited programs often meet higher standards of education and training.

Curriculum and Training: Review the curriculum of the barbering school or apprenticeship. Look for programs that offer comprehensive training in various cutting and styling techniques, grooming services, customer service, and relevant health and safety practices.

Visit the School or Shop: If possible, visit the barbering school or barbershop where the apprenticeship takes place. Observe the learning environment, facilities, and interactions between instructors and students or barbers and apprentices.

Talk to Current and Past Students/Apprentices: Reach out to current or former students of the school or apprenticeship program to get their firsthand experiences. Their insights can provide valuable information about the quality of education or training offered.

Instructors or Mentors: Learn about the qualifications and experiences of the instructors or barbers who will be teaching or mentoring you. Experienced and knowledgeable mentors can greatly influence your learning journey.

Placement Assistance: If you're considering a barbering school, inquire about their job placement assistance after completing the program. Some schools might have connections with local barbershops, which can be beneficial in starting your career.

Consider Location and Schedule: Evaluate the location and schedule of the school or apprenticeship program. Choose a location that is convenient for you and a schedule that fits your availability and lifestyle.

Financial Considerations: Compare tuition fees and costs associated with the program. If you're considering an apprenticeship, discuss the financial arrangements with the barbershop owner or mentor.

Reviews and Testimonials: Look for online reviews and testimonials from students or apprentices who have completed the program. Positive feedback can provide additional assurance about the quality of the school or apprenticeship.

Trust Your Instincts: Ultimately, trust your instincts when making a decision. Choose a program or apprenticeship that resonates with your goals, values, and aspirations as a future barber.

By conducting thorough research and considering these factors, you can increase the likelihood of choosing the right barbering school or apprenticeship that aligns with your career objectives and sets you on the path to success in the industry.

2b. Essential Tools And Equipment For Barbers

Barbers rely on a variety of tools and equipment to provide quality grooming services. Here are some essential tools commonly used by barbers:

Clippers: Professional hair clippers are a must-have for barbers. They come with various attachments for different hair lengths and styles.

Trimmers: Trimmers, also known as edgers or detailers, are used for precise cutting around the hairline, beard, and mustache.

Shears/Scissors: High-quality barber shears or scissors are essential for cutting and shaping hair with precision.

Razor: A straight razor or safety razor is used for clean shaves, beard sculpting, and detailing facial hair.

Comb: A durable and anti-static barber comb helps in sectioning and styling hair effectively.

Brushes: Barber brushes are used for cleaning hair clippings, as well as for styling and blending hair.

Barber Cape/Gown: A cape or gown is draped around the client's neck to protect their clothing during haircuts and grooming services.

Barber Chair: A comfortable and adjustable barber chair allows clients to sit comfortably during their service.

Barber Station: The barber station typically includes a mirror, storage for tools, and a workspace for the barber.

Neck Strips: Disposable neck strips are used to maintain hygiene and prevent hair from falling on the client's neck.

Disinfectants and Sanitizers: Barbers need disinfectants and sanitizers to maintain a clean and hygienic workspace, tools, and equipment.

Hair Products: A variety of hair products, such as pomades, gels, and waxes, are used for styling and finishing haircuts.

Towels and Neck Dusters: Towels are used for cleaning and drying hair, while neck dusters help remove loose hair from the neck and shoulders.

Hot Towel Steamer: A hot towel steamer is used to provide relaxing and pre-shave treatments.

Neck Strips: Disposable neck strips are used to maintain hygiene and prevent hair from falling on the client's neck.

Styling Products: Barbers use a range of hair styling products like pomades, gels, and waxes to achieve various looks.

Hair Dryer: A professional hair dryer helps in setting and styling hair quickly.

Styling Razor: A styling razor with disposable blades is used for creating texture and softening hair edges.

Clipper Guards: Attachable clipper guards or guide combs enable barbers to achieve consistent hair lengths during haircuts.

Shaving Cream and Aftershave: These are used during shaving services to provide a smooth shave and soothe the skin afterward.

Having the right tools and equipment is crucial for a barber to deliver excellent grooming services efficiently and professionally. Investing in high-quality tools and maintaining them properly will contribute to a successful barbering career.

2c. Setting Up Your Barber Shop Or Workstation

Setting up your barbershop or workstation requires careful planning and attention to detail. Here are some steps to help you create an organized and inviting space for your clients:

Location: Choose a location that is easily accessible to your target clientele. Consider areas with high foot traffic or near other businesses that can attract potential customers.

Licensing and Permits: Ensure you have obtained all the necessary licenses and permits to operate a barbershop legally in your area.

Design and Layout: Plan the layout of your barbershop, keeping in mind the flow of clients and the functionality of the workspace. Create separate areas for cutting, washing, and waiting, if possible.

Barber Station: Invest in quality barber chairs and set up each station with all the essential tools and equipment, including clippers, trimmers, shears, mirrors, and combs. Make sure there's enough space for your clients to feel comfortable during their service.

Waiting Area: Create a comfortable and inviting waiting area for your clients. Provide seating, magazines, and perhaps a TV to keep them entertained while they wait.

Storage and Organization: Keep your workspace tidy and organized by having ample storage for tools, products, and supplies. Use shelves, drawers, or cabinets to store items neatly.

Lighting: Ensure you have sufficient lighting at each barber station to see details clearly while cutting and styling hair.

Decor: Choose a theme or style for your barbershop that reflects your brand and appeals to your target audience. Consider using colors, decor, and artwork that create a welcoming atmosphere.

Amenities: Offer amenities that enhance the client experience, such as complimentary beverages or Wi-Fi.

Sanitation and Hygiene: Maintain a clean and hygienic environment. Regularly sanitize tools, chairs, and common areas to ensure the safety of your clients and staff.

Signage: Place clear and attractive signage both inside and outside your barbershop to attract potential clients and inform them about your services.

Payment System: Set up a convenient and secure payment system for your clients. Accept various payment methods, including cash, credit/debit cards, and mobile payments.

Marketing and Branding: Develop a strong brand identity and use marketing strategies to promote your barbershop. Utilize social media, a website, and local advertising to reach potential clients.

Customer Service: Train your staff, if applicable, in excellent customer service to ensure clients feel valued and satisfied with their experience.

Remember that your barbershop's setup and atmosphere play a significant role in attracting and retaining clients. By creating a comfortable and professional environment, you can build a loyal clientele and establish a successful barbershop business.

* * *

CHAPTER 3: MASTERING BARBERING TECHNIQUES

3a. Haircutting Fundamentals And Different Cutting Styles

To learn the haircutting fundamentals in different styles, you can follow these steps:

Research Online: Look for haircutting tutorials, guides, and resources online. There are numerous videos and articles available that demonstrate various haircutting techniques for different styles.

Barbering Books: Invest in barbering books written by experienced professionals. These books often provide step-by-step instructions and illustrations for various haircutting styles.

Barbering Schools or Courses: Enroll in a reputable barbering school or take online courses that offer comprehensive training in haircutting techniques. Qualified instructors can guide you through the fundamentals of different styles.

Attend Workshops and Seminars: Look for haircutting workshops and seminars conducted by experienced barbers or hairstylists. These events provide hands-on experience and insights into specific styles.

Seek Mentorship: If possible, find a seasoned barber willing to mentor and teach you different haircutting styles. Learning from someone with practical experience can be invaluable.

Practice on Mannequins: Practice haircutting on mannequin heads to build your skills and confidence. This allows you to experiment with various techniques without the pressure of working on real clients.

Observe Experienced Barbers: Visit barbershops and observe experienced barbers at work. Pay attention to their techniques, approaches, and the tools they use for different haircutting styles.

Online Communities and Forums: Join barbering forums and social media groups where professionals share tips and insights. Engaging with others in the community can provide valuable learning opportunities.

Follow Barbering Influencers: Follow renowned barbers and hairstylists on social media platforms. They often share haircutting tutorials and tips that can help you learn about different styles.

Attend Trade Shows: Visit barbering trade shows and events, where you can witness live demonstrations and gain exposure to the latest haircutting trends and techniques.

Practice, Practice, Practice: The key to mastering haircutting fundamentals is consistent practice. Work on friends, family members, or volunteer models to apply what you've learned.

Remember, learning different haircutting styles requires time and dedication. Start with the basics and gradually move on to more advanced techniques. Be patient with yourself and continuously seek opportunities to improve your skills through learning and hands-on experience.

3b. The Art Of Using Scissors, Clippers, And Razors

Mastering the art of using scissors, clippers, and razors in barbering requires dedication, practice, and continuous learning. Here are some steps to help you improve your skills:

Education and Training: Enroll in a reputable barbering school or take specialized courses that focus on scissor, clipper, and razor techniques. Formal education can provide a solid foundation and exposure to various cutting styles.

Understand Tools and Techniques: Study the different types of scissors, clippers, and razors available in the market, along with their specific uses and functions. Learn the various cutting techniques for different hair textures and styles.

Practice on Mannequins: Begin practicing haircutting techniques on mannequin heads to hone your skills. Mannequins allow you to experiment without the pressure of working on real clients.

Seek Guidance from Experienced Barbers: If possible, find an experienced barber who can mentor you and provide feedback on your cutting techniques. Observing professionals at work can be a valuable learning experience.

Attend Workshops and Seminars: Participate in haircutting workshops and seminars conducted by skilled barbers. These events often include hands-on practice and demonstrations.

Watch Online Tutorials: Utilize online resources, such as videos and tutorials, to learn new cutting techniques and gain insights from expert barbers.

Focus on Fundamentals: Master the basic haircutting techniques before moving on to more complex styles. Understanding the fundamentals is essential for building a strong foundation.

Practice Patience: Improving your skills takes time and patience. Be willing to make mistakes and learn from them as you progress in your barbering journey.

Seek Feedback: Request feedback from friends, family, or colleagues who act as models for your haircuts. Constructive criticism can help you identify areas for improvement.

Attend Barber Competitions: Participate in or attend barber competitions to see the work of talented professionals and gain inspiration for your own skills.

Keep Up with Trends: Stay updated with the latest trends in barbering by following industry magazines, social media accounts of influential barbers, and attending trade shows.

Experiment and Be Creative: Don't be afraid to experiment with different cutting techniques and be creative in your approach. Developing your unique style sets you apart as a skilled barber.

Remember, mastering the use of scissors, clippers, and razors in barbering is a continuous journey of learning and improvement. Stay dedicated to your craft, practice regularly, and seek opportunities for growth to become a skilled and accomplished barber.

3c. Beard Grooming And Facial Hair Design

Mastering the art of beard grooming and facial hair design in barbering requires a combination of technical skills, creativity, and attention to detail.

Here are some steps to help you become proficient in this aspect of barbering:

Learn Beard Anatomy: Understand the different parts of the beard, such as the neckline, cheek line, and mustache, and how they contribute to shaping the overall look.

Practice Basic Techniques: Start with the fundamentals of beard grooming, such as trimming, shaping, and blending. Practice on willing models to gain experience.

Study Different Facial Hair Styles: Familiarize yourself with various beard styles and facial hair designs, from classic to modern trends. Learn the techniques required for each style.

Invest in Quality Tools: Use high-quality trimmers, scissors, and razors designed for beard grooming. Proper tools are essential for achieving precise and clean results.

Seek Mentorship: If possible, find an experienced barber who specializes in beard grooming and facial hair design. Learning from a mentor can provide valuable insights and tips.

Attend Beard Grooming Workshops: Look for workshops or seminars focused on beard grooming techniques. Hands-on practice under the guidance of experts can accelerate your learning.

Learn Face Shapes: Understand how different face shapes influence beard styles and design. Tailor your approach to suit each client's unique features.

Communication with Clients: Listen carefully to your clients' preferences and take their input into account when designing their facial hair. Good communication ensures client satisfaction.

Study Beard Products: Familiarize yourself with various beard products like beard oils, balms, and waxes. Learn how to use them to enhance and maintain the beard's appearance.

Stay Updated with Trends: Follow beard grooming trends and styles through online resources, magazines, and social media accounts dedicated to men's grooming.

Experiment and Practice: Experiment with different techniques and styles on models to improve your skills. The more you practice, the more confident you'll become in creating unique facial hair designs.

Attention to Detail: Pay attention to small details, such as symmetry, balance, and neatness, as they can significantly impact the final look of the beard.

Build a Portfolio: Document your best beard grooming work in a portfolio to showcase your skills to potential clients and employers.

Receive Feedback: Seek feedback from clients and colleagues to identify areas for improvement and refine your techniques.

By following these steps and dedicating time and effort to mastering beard grooming and facial hair design, you can become a sought-after barber known for your expertise in creating impressive and stylish facial hair looks.

* * *

CHAPTER 4: THE ART OF COMMUNICATION

4a. Building Strong Client Relationships

Building strong client relationships in barbering is crucial for a successful and sustainable career. Here are some effective ways to strengthen your bond with clients:

Active Listening: Practice active listening during consultations. Pay attention to your clients' preferences, concerns, and expectations, and show genuine interest in their needs.

Personalize Services: Tailor your services to each client's unique style and preferences. Remember their favorite haircuts, beard styles, and any specific grooming requests.

Remember Names: Address clients by their names to create a more personalized experience. Remembering names shows that you value and respect them as individuals.

Maintain Consistency: Strive to deliver consistent and high-quality services with each visit. Clients appreciate knowing they can rely on you for a great experience every time.

Provide Excellent Customer Service: Go the extra mile to ensure your clients feel comfortable and well-cared for during their time in your barbershop. Offer them a warm welcome, refreshments, and a clean and inviting environment.

Be Professional and Punctual: Respect your clients' time by staying on schedule and being punctual. Maintain a professional demeanor and appearance at all times.

Communication: Keep the lines of communication open with your clients. Ask for feedback after each service, and encourage them to share any concerns or suggestions.

Follow Up: After a service, follow up with clients to check how they're doing with their new haircut or beard style. A simple message shows that you care about their satisfaction.

Reward Loyalty: Implement a loyalty program or offer special promotions to reward clients for their continued patronage.

Stay Engaged on Social Media: Connect with clients on social media platforms to share updates, haircare tips, and style inspirations. Engaging online can reinforce your relationship beyond the barbershop.

Be Personable: Show your personality and let clients get to know you. A friendly and approachable demeanor can make clients feel more comfortable and build rapport.

Handle Complaints Professionally: If a client expresses dissatisfaction, handle the situation professionally and empathetically. Address their concerns and work toward a satisfactory resolution.

Offer Grooming Tips: Provide grooming tips and advice to help clients maintain their hair and facial hair between visits. This adds value to your services and shows you care about their appearance.

Stay Updated on Trends: Keep abreast of the latest grooming and hairstyling trends to offer fresh and relevant suggestions to clients.

Building strong client relationships in barbering is an ongoing process that requires genuine care, attention, and consistent effort. By focusing on providing exceptional service and personalized experiences, you can cultivate loyal and satisfied clients who return to your barbershop time and time again.

4b. Effective Communication And Active Listening

Effective communication and active listening are of utmost importance in barbering. They play a significant role in building strong client relationships and providing excellent grooming services. Here's why they are crucial:

Understanding Client Preferences: Effective communication allows barbers to understand their clients' preferences, style choices, and specific grooming needs. By actively listening to clients during consultations, barbers can deliver haircuts and facial hair designs that align with their clients' desires.

Creating Personalized Experiences: By actively engaging with clients, barbers can create personalized grooming experiences. Knowing their clients' preferences and addressing any concerns ensures that clients feel valued and well-cared for during their visit.

Building Trust: Trust is essential in the barber-client relationship. When clients feel heard and understood, they are more likely to trust their barber's recommendations and expertise.

Avoiding Misunderstandings: Miscommunication can lead to unsatisfactory results or misunderstandings. Effective communication helps barbers clarify their clients' expectations, ensuring both parties are on the same page.

Enhancing Customer Satisfaction: When clients feel that their barber has genuinely listened to their needs and preferences, they are more likely to leave the barbershop satisfied with their grooming service.

Addressing Concerns: Active listening enables barbers to identify any concerns or issues that clients may have with their haircuts or facial hair designs. Addressing these concerns promptly can prevent dissatisfaction and build client loyalty.

Providing Tailored Advice: By listening to clients' questions or concerns about hair and facial hair maintenance, barbers can offer tailored advice and product recommendations to help clients maintain their grooming between visits.

Improving Client Retention: Barber-client relationships built on effective communication and active listening tend to result in higher client retention rates. Satisfied clients are more likely to return to the same barber for future grooming needs.

Enhancing Word-of-Mouth Referrals: Happy clients are more inclined to recommend their barber to friends and family. Positive word-of-mouth referrals are invaluable for growing a successful barbering business.

Building a Positive Reputation: Barbers who excel in communication and active listening are more likely to build a positive reputation in the community. A good reputation attracts new clients and contributes to the long-term success of the barbershop.

In summary, effective communication and active listening are essential for a successful career in barbering. By valuing client input, understanding their needs, and providing personalized services, barbers can foster strong relationships, build trust, and ensure client satisfaction.

4c. Managing Client Expectations And Preferences

Managing client expectations and preferences in barbering is essential to ensure a positive and satisfactory experience for your clients. Here are some effective ways to handle this:

Active Consultation: Begin each appointment with an active consultation. Take the time to listen attentively to your client's preferences, style choices, and any specific requests they may have for their haircut or facial hair design.

Show Visual References: Use visual aids such as pictures or style guides to help your clients express their desired look more clearly. This can prevent misinterpretations and ensure you both have a clear understanding of the end result.

Offer Honest Feedback: Provide professional feedback and recommendations based on your expertise. If a requested style may not suit the client's face shape or hair texture, gently suggest alternatives that would be more flattering.

Discuss Realistic Results: Be transparent with your clients about what can be achieved based on their hair type, length, and condition. Managing expectations regarding potential outcomes can prevent disappointments.

Educate Clients: Offer insights into haircare and grooming practices that can help your clients maintain their desired look between visits. Educating them on styling techniques and product usage can be valuable.

Set Clear Boundaries: Establish boundaries around the services you provide. Let clients know what you can and cannot do, especially if their request falls outside your area of expertise.

Showcase Your Portfolio: Display a portfolio of your work or share photos of your previous clients' transformations. This can help clients understand the range of styles you excel at and build confidence in your skills.

Time Management: Allocate adequate time for each client to avoid rushing through appointments. This allows you to focus on meeting their expectations and providing a quality service.

Manage Wait Times: Minimize wait times to prevent clients from becoming impatient or frustrated. Respect their time by adhering to your schedule.

Maintain Open Communication: Encourage clients to provide feedback after each service and remain approachable if they have questions or concerns. Responding positively to feedback shows that you value their input.

Stay Updated on Trends: Keep up with the latest grooming and hairstyling trends to offer relevant suggestions to clients who may seek a change in their look.

Monitor Client Preferences: Take notes on your clients' preferences, style choices, and any specific requests. This helps you remember their preferences for future visits.

By employing these strategies, you can effectively manage client expectations and preferences in barbering. Creating a positive and comfortable atmosphere for communication will enhance client satisfaction and contribute to a loyal and happy clientele.

* * *

CHAPTER 5: DEVELOPING YOUR BARBERING SKILLS

5a. Continuous Learning And Professional Development

Continuous learning and professional development are highly important in the field of barbering. Here's why they are crucial for a barber's success:

Staying Updated with Trends: The grooming industry is ever-evolving, with new haircuts, beard styles, and grooming techniques emerging regularly. Continuous learning allows barbers to stay current with the latest trends, ensuring they can offer modern and in-demand services to their clients.

Improving Technical Skills: Regularly seeking opportunities for professional development helps barbers improve their technical skills. This includes mastering various haircutting and beard grooming techniques, which are essential for providing high-quality services.

Adapting to Client Preferences: Clients' preferences can change over time, and what's popular today may be different tomorrow. Continuous learning allows barbers to adapt to shifting client preferences, ensuring they can meet the unique needs of their clientele.

Building Confidence: The more a barber learns and practices new techniques, the more confident they become in their abilities. Confidence in their skills translates to better customer service and greater client satisfaction.

Learning New Products and Tools: Continuous learning exposes barbers to new grooming products and tools, such as specialized clippers or beard oils. Understanding how to use and recommend these products enhances the overall client experience.

Networking and Collaboration: Attending industry events and workshops allows barbers to network with peers and industry professionals. Collaboration and sharing experiences with others can lead to valuable insights and opportunities for growth.

Expanding Services Offered: Learning new techniques and skills enables barbers to expand their service offerings. For example, a barber who specializes in traditional haircuts might consider learning modern fades or beard sculpting to attract a broader clientele.

Enhancing Business Growth: A barber who invests in continuous learning demonstrates a commitment to their profession. This dedication can attract more clients and contribute to the growth of their business.

Meeting Industry Standards: The grooming industry has certain standards and best practices. Continuous learning ensures that barbers are knowledgeable about industry regulations and can maintain a high level of professionalism.

Fostering Passion for the Craft: Learning and exploring new aspects of barbering can reignite a barber's passion for the craft. The pursuit of knowledge can lead to a deeper appreciation for their profession.

In summary, continuous learning and professional development are essential for barbers to stay relevant, provide top-notch services, and remain competitive in the industry. It's an ongoing journey of improvement that fosters growth, confidence, and a deeper connection to the art and practice of barbering.

5b. Attending Workshops, Seminars, And Industry Events

Attending workshops, seminars, and industry events is highly important for barbers, and here's why:

Skill Enhancement: Workshops and seminars offer hands-on training and demonstrations by experienced professionals. They provide an opportunity to learn new techniques, refine existing skills, and stay updated with the latest trends in the industry.

Networking Opportunities: Industry events bring together barbers, hairstylists, and grooming experts from various backgrounds. Networking at these events can lead to valuable connections, collaborations, and potential job opportunities.

Exposure to New Products and Tools: Manufacturers often showcase new grooming products and tools at industry events. Attending these events allows barbers to test and learn about innovative products that can enhance their services.

Inspiration and Motivation: Being in a space with other passionate professionals can be inspiring and motivating. Seeing the work of talented barbers and hearing success stories can encourage barbers to continue honing their craft.

Professional Development: Many workshops and seminars offer certifications or continuing education credits, which contribute to a barber's professional development and may be required for certain licensing or accreditation.

Learning from Industry Experts: Workshops and seminars are typically conducted by industry experts who have valuable insights and knowledge to share. Learning from the best can significantly improve a barber's skillset.

Keeping Up with Industry Trends: The grooming industry is constantly evolving, with new haircutting styles and grooming techniques emerging regularly. Attending industry events helps barbers stay current with the latest trends and innovations.

Building Confidence: Acquiring new knowledge and skills through workshops and seminars builds a barber's confidence in their abilities. Confident barbers are more likely to provide exceptional services and have satisfied clients.

Brand Exposure: For barbershop owners, attending industry events can offer brand exposure and help establish the barbershop as a reputable and forward-thinking business.

Continuing Education: Barbering is a profession that requires continuous learning to remain relevant and competitive. Workshops and seminars provide a structured way to continue education and stay at the forefront of the industry.

In conclusion, attending workshops, seminars, and industry events is highly beneficial for barbers as it fosters skill development, expands professional networks, and keeps them abreast of industry trends. It is an investment in both personal and professional growth, contributing to a successful and fulfilling career in barbering.

5c. Exploring Creative Expression In Barbering

Exploring creative expression in barbering allows you to showcase your unique style and artistic vision. Here arc some ways to nurture your creativity in the field:

Experiment with Hair Designs: Try different haircut and beard designs that go beyond the traditional styles. Use your artistic flair to create innovative and eye-catching looks for your clients.

Follow Barbering Influencers: Follow social media accounts and websites of renowned barbers who showcase creative and unconventional styles. Draw inspiration from their work and adapt it to your own unique approach.

Participate in Barber Competitions: Enter local or national barber competitions that focus on creativity and design. Competing will challenge you to push the boundaries of your skills and creativity.

Attend Workshops and Seminars: Enroll in workshops or seminars that specifically explore creative aspects of barbering. Learn from industry experts and practice new techniques.

Collaborate with Other Artists: Collaborate with hairstylists, photographers, or makeup artists on creative projects. Cross-disciplinary collaborations can spark new ideas and expand your artistic horizons.

Offer Themed Grooming Events: Host themed grooming events or pop-up shops that allow you to showcase your creative work and attract clients interested in unique styles.

Incorporate Hair Color: Experiment with hair color and highlights to add a creative twist to your haircuts and designs. Properly executed hair color can elevate your work to new artistic levels.

Utilize Different Tools and Techniques: Explore various cutting tools, such as razors, texturizing shears, and clipper art, to add artistic elements to your haircuts and beard designs.

Create a Portfolio: Document your most creative work in a portfolio to showcase your skills to potential clients or employers. A portfolio serves as a visual representation of your creative abilities.

Take Inspiration from Art and Fashion: Look to art, fashion, and pop culture for inspiration. Draw on different artistic styles and trends to infuse creativity into your grooming work.

Personalize Consultations: Engage in detailed consultations with clients to understand their personality, lifestyle, and preferences. Use this information to create personalized, creative styles that reflect their individuality.

Embrace Unconventional Techniques: Don't be afraid to explore unconventional cutting techniques or layering methods to achieve unique and artistic looks.

Remember, creativity in barbering is about thinking outside the box and using your skills to create extraordinary and personalized grooming experiences for your clients. Embrace experimentation and stay open to new ideas to continuously nurture your creative expression in the field.

* * *

CHAPTER 6: BUSINESS AND MARKETING STRATEGIES

6a. Creating A Successful Business Plan For Your Barber Shop

Creating a successful business plan for your barbershop is a critical step in setting a clear direction for your venture and attracting potential investors or lenders. Here's a step-by-step guide to help you develop an effective business plan:

Executive Summary: Start with a concise overview of your barbershop business, including the vision, mission, target market, and key objectives. Keep this section brief but impactful, as it serves as an introduction to your business.

Company Description: Provide detailed information about your barbershop, such as its legal structure (sole proprietorship, partnership, LLC, etc.), location, services offered, and unique selling points that set it apart from competitors.

Market Analysis: Conduct thorough research on your target market, local demographics, and competitors. Understand the demand for barbering services in your area and identify your primary competitors' strengths and weaknesses.

Marketing and Sales Strategies: Outline your marketing and sales plans to attract clients and build brand awareness. Include details about advertising, promotions, social media, and any partnerships or collaborations.

Services and Pricing: Clearly define the grooming services you will offer and set competitive pricing based on your market research. Consider bundling services or offering loyalty programs to attract and retain clients.

Organization and Management: Provide an overview of your barbershop's organizational structure, including the management team's roles and responsibilities. Mention any relevant industry experience or certifications of key personnel.

Financial Projections: Create realistic financial projections for the first three to five years of your barbershop's operation. Include sales forecasts, expense estimates, and projected profits. Make sure your financial assumptions are well-supported.

Funding Request (if applicable): If you need external funding, specify the amount required and the purpose of the funds. Clearly state how you plan to use the investment to grow your business.

Operational Plan: Detail the day-to-day operations of your barbershop, including working hours, staffing requirements, and inventory management.

Risk Assessment: Identify potential risks and challenges your barbershop may face and outline strategies to mitigate them. These could include factors like changing market conditions, local competition, or staffing issues.

Exit Strategy: Include an exit strategy, even if you don't plan to leave the business anytime soon. It demonstrates foresight and is valuable for potential investors.

Executive Summary (Revisited): End your business plan with a concise summary that reiterates the key points, goals, and highlights the potential for success.

Remember, a well-structured business plan serves as a roadmap for your barbershop's success and helps you stay focused on your objectives. Regularly revisit and update your business plan as your barbershop grows and evolves.

6b. Marketing Your Services And Building A Loyal Clientele

Building a loyal clientele and effectively marketing your barber services go hand in hand. Here are some strategies to help you achieve both:

Create an Online Presence: Build a professional website and establish a presence on social media platforms. Share photos of your work, engage with followers, and post informative content related to grooming tips and trends.

Offer Promotions and Loyalty Programs: Attract new clients and encourage repeat business by offering promotions, discounts, or loyalty programs. Rewarding loyal customers can foster long-term relationships.

Ask for Referrals: Encourage satisfied clients to refer friends and family to your barbershop. Word-of-mouth referrals are powerful and can help you reach a broader audience.

Engage with the Local Community: Participate in local events or collaborate with nearby businesses to gain visibility and connect with potential clients in the area.

Online Reviews and Testimonials: Positive online reviews and testimonials build trust and credibility. Encourage satisfied clients to leave reviews on platforms like Google My Business or Yelp.

Host Events or Workshops: Organize grooming workshops, themed events, or barbering demonstrations to showcase your skills and attract new clients.

Offer Exceptional Customer Service: Provide a memorable and enjoyable experience to every client. Personalized service and attention to detail can leave a lasting impression.

Use Visuals to Showcase Your Work: Share high-quality images and videos of your haircuts and grooming services on social media to highlight your expertise and creativity.

Stay Updated with Trends: Continuously learn about new grooming trends and techniques to offer fresh and fashionable services to your clients.

Collaborate with Influencers: Partner with local influencers or social media personalities to reach a broader audience and gain exposure for your barbershop.

Respond to Inquiries Promptly: Respond promptly to phone calls, emails, or messages from potential clients. Being attentive shows professionalism and customer care.

Network with Other Local Businesses: Connect with nearby businesses, such as salons, clothing boutiques, or gyms, to cross-promote services and refer clients to each other.

Maintain a Clean and Inviting Barbershop: A clean and comfortable environment is crucial for a positive client experience. Ensure your barbershop reflects professionalism and hygiene.

Celebrate Client Milestones: Acknowledge client birthdays, anniversaries, or other special occasions to make them feel valued and appreciated.

Remember, building a loyal clientele takes time and consistent effort. By providing top-notch services, actively engaging with your community, and showcasing your skills through various marketing channels, you can attract new clients and keep them coming back to your barbershop for years to come.

6c. Utilizing Social Media And Online Presence To Attract Clients

Utilizing social media and creating a strong online presence are powerful tools to attract clients to your barber business. Here's how you can make the most of social media to promote your services:

Choose the Right Platforms: Identify the social media platforms most relevant to your target audience. Instagram and Facebook are popular choices for visual content and engaging with clients.

Create a Professional Profile: Set up a business account on your chosen platforms. Use a clear profile picture and write a concise and compelling bio that showcases your expertise and services.

Showcase Your Work: Share high-quality images and videos of your haircuts, beard designs, and grooming services. Visuals are essential for attracting potential clients and demonstrating your skills.

Engage with Followers: Respond to comments, messages, and inquiries promptly. Engaging with your followers builds a sense of community and trust.

Post Consistently: Maintain a regular posting schedule to keep your audience engaged. Share grooming tips, behind-the-scenes content, and updates about your barbershop.

Utilize Hashtags: Use relevant hashtags in your posts to reach a broader audience and connect with people interested in grooming and barbering.

Run Contests and Giveaways: Organize contests or giveaways to encourage interaction and attract new followers. Offering free grooming sessions or products can generate excitement and interest.

Collaborate with Influencers: Partner with local influencers or social media personalities in your area to promote your services and reach a larger audience.

Share Client Testimonials: Share positive reviews or testimonials from satisfied clients to build trust and credibility.

Promote Special Offers: Announce special promotions or discounts exclusively for your social media followers to incentivize them to book appointments.

Share Before-and-After Transformations: Highlight the transformations your clients undergo after their grooming sessions. Before-and-after photos are attention-grabbing and showcase your skills.

Utilize Stories and Reels: Use Instagram Stories and Reels to provide quick grooming tips, showcase your personality, and share behind-the-scenes content.

Interact with Local Businesses: Engage with other local businesses, organizations, or events on social media. Collaborating or cross-promoting can introduce your services to a wider audience.

Encourage User-Generated Content: Encourage clients to share their post-grooming selfies and tag your barbershop. User-generated content serves as free advertising and social proof.

Remember, consistency and authenticity are key to building a successful online presence. Stay active on social media, be genuine in your interactions, and showcase your passion for barbering. As you continue to engage with your audience and share valuable content, you'll attract more clients and establish your barbershop as a reputable and sought-after grooming destination.

* * *

CHAPTER 7: PROVIDING TOP-NOTCH CUSTOMER SERVICE

7a. Ensuring A Positive Customer Experience

Ensuring a positive customer experience is essential for building a loyal clientele and establishing a successful barbering business. Here are some tips to create a memorable and enjoyable experience for your clients:

Active Listening: Pay close attention to your clients during consultations. Listen to their preferences, concerns, and desired outcomes for their haircut or grooming service.

Friendly and Welcoming Atmosphere: Greet clients warmly when they arrive and create a comfortable and inviting environment in your barbershop.

Personalized Service: Tailor your services to each client's unique needs and style preferences. Treat every client as an individual and make them feel valued.

Communicate Clearly: Explain the haircutting or grooming process to your clients, and be transparent about the techniques you'll use. Set clear expectations to avoid misunderstandings.

Offer Professional Recommendations: Provide expert advice and recommendations based on your knowledge and experience. Offer hairstyle or beard design suggestions that suit your clients' facial features and hair type.

Be Respectful of Time: Respect your clients' time by starting appointments on schedule and avoiding unnecessary delays.

Maintain Cleanliness and Hygiene: Keep your workspace and tools clean and sanitized. Clients appreciate a high level of hygiene and professionalism.

Provide Comfort: Ensure your clients are comfortable during their visit. Offer them a beverage, a clean cape, and a comfortable chair during their grooming session.

Engage in Conversation: Establish rapport with your clients through friendly conversation, but also be mindful of their cues if they prefer a more relaxed, quiet experience.

Offering Refreshments: Consider providing complimentary refreshments like water, coffee, or tea to enhance the customer experience.

Attention to Detail: Pay attention to the finer points of your clients' haircuts or beard designs. Neatly finish the details to ensure a polished and refined look.

Handle Complaints Professionally: If a client expresses dissatisfaction, handle the situation with professionalism and empathy. Address their concerns and work toward a resolution.

Follow-Up: After their visit, follow up with clients to ensure they are satisfied with their haircut or grooming service. Showing that you care about their experience builds trust.

Offering Aftercare Tips: Provide clients with aftercare tips and product recommendations to maintain their hairstyle or beard at home.

By focusing on these aspects of customer experience, you can leave a positive impression on your clients, encourage repeat business, and attract word-of-mouth referrals. Satisfied clients are more likely to become loyal supporters of your barbering business and contribute to its success.

7b. Handling Difficult Situations And Customer Complaints

Handling difficult situations and customer complaints with professionalism and empathy is crucial for maintaining a positive reputation as a barber. Here's the best way to approach such situations:

Stay Calm and Composed: Remain composed and avoid becoming defensive or confrontational. Take a deep breath and focus on understanding the client's concerns.

Listen Actively: Give the client your full attention and actively listen to their complaint without interrupting. Let them express their feelings and thoughts.

Empathize with the Customer: Show empathy by acknowledging the client's feelings and frustrations. Let them know that you understand their perspective and that their feedback is valuable.

Apologize Sincerely: Apologize for any inconvenience or dissatisfaction the client experienced. A sincere apology can go a long way in diffusing the situation.

Ask for Specifics: Ask the client to provide specific details about what they didn't like or what went wrong. Understanding the exact issue can help you address it effectively.

Offer Solutions: Propose solutions to resolve the problem and ask the client how they would like the issue to be resolved. Be willing to accommodate reasonable requests.

Avoid Blame-Shifting: Refrain from blaming others or making excuses. Focus on finding a solution rather than dwelling on who is at fault.

Rectify the Issue: Take immediate action to correct the problem or concern. If possible, offer to redo the haircut or grooming service to the client's satisfaction.

Follow Up: After resolving the issue, follow up with the client to ensure they are now satisfied with the resolution. This shows that you genuinely care about their experience.

Learn from the Feedback: Use the feedback as an opportunity for self-improvement. Consider whether there are areas in your services that can be enhanced to prevent similar issues in the future.

Maintain Professionalism: Throughout the process, maintain a professional and courteous demeanor. Treat the client with respect, even if the situation becomes challenging.

Document the Complaint: Document the details of the complaint, how it was resolved, and the steps taken to prevent similar issues in the future. This documentation can be valuable for learning and training purposes.

Use Feedback to Improve: Use customer complaints as constructive feedback to improve your services and enhance the overall customer experience.

Remember, handling customer complaints effectively can turn a dissatisfied client into a loyal supporter of your barbering business. Your professionalism, empathy, and willingness to address concerns can leave a lasting positive impression on your clients and contribute to a strong reputation in the industry.

7c. Going The Extra Mile To Exceed Client Expectations

Exceeding client expectations is a great way to build strong relationships and foster customer loyalty. Here are some ways to go the extra mile as a barber and leave a lasting impression on your clients:

Personalized Consultations: Conduct thorough consultations to understand your clients' style preferences, lifestyle, and grooming needs. Tailor your services to their unique requirements.

Attention to Detail: Pay close attention to the small details of a haircut or beard design. Neatly finish edges and ensure a precise and polished look.

Offer Complimentary Services: Surprise your clients with complimentary services, such as a relaxing scalp massage, hot towel treatment, or a beard oil application.

Anticipate Needs: Anticipate your clients' needs and preferences based on previous visits. Remember their favorite haircuts or grooming products to create a personalized experience.

Provide Expert Advice: Offer expert advice on haircare and grooming techniques. Educate your clients on how to maintain their hairstyle or beard between visits.

Create a Comfortable Environment: Ensure your barbershop is clean, inviting, and well-maintained. Provide comfortable seating and a pleasant atmosphere for your clients.

Follow-Up: After the service, follow up with your clients to check how they are doing with their haircut or grooming. A simple message or phone call shows that you care about their satisfaction.

Remember Special Occasions: Take note of your clients' special occasions, such as birthdays or anniversaries, and acknowledge them with a thoughtful gesture or discount.

Offer Refreshments: Provide complimentary refreshments like water, coffee, or tea to make your clients feel welcomed and pampered.

Stay Updated with Trends: Continuously improve your skills and stay updated with the latest grooming trends to offer fresh and fashionable services.

Share Before-and-After Photos: Show clients before-and-after photos of their transformation. Visual evidence of your work can be impressive and appreciated.

Surprise Discounts or Rewards: Surprise clients with occasional discounts, loyalty rewards, or referral bonuses to express your gratitude for their continued support.

Ask for Feedback: Request feedback from your clients regularly to understand their needs better and find areas for improvement.

Thank-You Notes: Send thank-you notes or messages to clients after their visits, expressing your appreciation for their patronage.

Remember that going the extra mile is not about extravagant gestures but rather about demonstrating your dedication to providing exceptional service and a memorable experience. By consistently exceeding client expectations, you can foster long-term client loyalty and establish a reputation as a go-to barber for top-notch grooming services.

* * *

CHAPTER 8: MAINTAINING A CLEAN AND SANITARY ENVIRONMENT

8a. Understanding The Importance Of Hygiene In Barbering

Understanding the importance of hygiene in barbering is crucial for providing a safe and professional environment for both barbers and clients. Here's why hygiene matters in the barbering industry:

Client Safety: Maintaining proper hygiene practices ensures that clients are protected from potential infections or cross-contamination during haircuts, beard trims, or other grooming services.

Preventing Infections: Proper hygiene, including sanitizing tools and workstations, helps prevent the spread of bacteria, viruses, and fungal infections between clients.

Professionalism: A clean and hygienic barbershop reflects professionalism and instills confidence in clients, enhancing their overall experience.

Client Trust: Clients are more likely to trust a barber who takes hygiene seriously. Trust is essential for building long-term client relationships and generating positive word-of-mouth referrals.

Compliance with Regulations: Adhering to hygiene standards and practices ensures that your barbershop complies with health and safety regulations set by local authorities.

Barber Health: Proper hygiene practices protect barbers from potential exposure to infectious agents, safeguarding their health and well-being.

Cleanliness Enhances Comfort: A clean and well-maintained barbershop environment creates a comfortable and pleasant experience for both barbers and clients.

Image and Reputation: A hygienic barbershop projects a positive image and reputation, attracting more clients and contributing to business growth.

Preventing Skin Irritation: Clean and sanitized tools, as well as proper cleaning of workstations, reduce the risk of skin irritation caused by residual hair or product buildup.

Hygiene Enhances Client Experience: A clean and organized barbershop environment, along with sanitized tools, contributes to a positive client experience, making them more likely to return for future services.

Protecting Vulnerable Clients: Some clients may have compromised immune systems or skin conditions, making proper hygiene practices essential for their safety and well-being.

Proper Disposal of Waste: Hygienic practices include the appropriate disposal of waste materials, such as used razor blades and single-use items, to prevent potential hazards.

Preventing Contamination of Products: Regularly cleaning and sanitizing product containers and dispensers helps prevent contamination of grooming products.

Adapting to COVID-19 and Other Health Concerns: In times of health crises or outbreaks, maintaining strict hygiene practices becomes even more critical to protect both clients and barbers.

In summary, hygiene is a fundamental aspect of barbering that ensures the safety, health, and well-being of both clients and barbers. By prioritizing cleanliness and following proper hygiene protocols, you create a professional, trustworthy, and inviting atmosphere that leaves a positive impression on clients and fosters long-term success for your barbershop.

8b. Sterilization And Disinfection Best Practices

Sterilization and disinfection are critical practices in the barbering industry to ensure the safety and well-being of clients and barbers. Here are the best practices to follow:

Clean and Organized Workspace: Maintain a clean and organized workspace free from clutter. Regularly clean countertops, chairs, and surfaces to prevent the buildup of dust and debris.

Hand Hygiene: Wash hands thoroughly with soap and water before and after each client interaction. Use hand sanitizers with at least 60% alcohol when handwashing facilities are not readily available.

Sterilize Tools: Properly sterilize all reusable tools, such as scissors, clippers, razors, and combs, after each use. Use an autoclave, dry heat sterilizer, or chemical solution approved for barbering tools.

Single-Use Items: Use single-use disposable items, such as disposable razors, neck strips, and cape liners, to avoid cross-contamination between clients.

Cleaning Haircutting Stations: Thoroughly clean and sanitize the haircutting stations between clients. Disinfect the chair, armrests, headrest, and any other surfaces that came in contact with the previous client.

Sanitize Clippers and Trimmers: Disassemble clippers and trimmers after each use to remove hair and debris. Sanitize the blades with a suitable clipper spray or wipe before using them on the next client.

Replace Neck Strips and Capes: Use fresh neck strips and capes for each client to prevent the transfer of hair and skin particles.

Sanitize Combs and Brushes: Clean and sanitize combs and brushes between clients using an approved disinfectant.

Sterilize Blades and Attachments: Sterilize detachable blades and clipper attachments in a disinfectant solution or with an approved sterilization method.

Provide Clean Towels: Use fresh and clean towels for each client. Do not reuse towels or share towels between clients.

Disinfect Waiting Areas: Regularly disinfect waiting areas, chairs, and any frequently touched surfaces to maintain a clean environment.

Use Disposable Gloves: Consider wearing disposable gloves during certain procedures, such as facial hair design or when applying grooming products.

Sanitize Cash Register and Payment Devices: Clean and sanitize the cash register, credit card terminals, and other payment devices regularly to prevent the spread of germs.

Follow Local Regulations: Comply with local health and safety regulations and guidelines related to sanitation and disinfection in the barbering industry.

By following these best practices in sterilization and disinfection, you demonstrate your commitment to maintaining a safe and hygienic environment for both clients and barbers. Prioritizing cleanliness and client safety builds trust and fosters a positive reputation for your barbershop.

8c. Creating A Safe And Welcoming Atmosphere For Clients

Creating a safe and welcoming atmosphere for clients is essential for building trust, loyalty, and positive word-of-mouth referrals. Here's the best way to achieve this as a barber:

Maintain Cleanliness: Keep your barbershop clean and well-organized. Regularly sanitize and disinfect all workstations, tools, and frequently touched surfaces.

Display Health and Safety Measures: Clearly communicate the health and safety measures you've implemented in response to COVID-19 or other health concerns. Post signs about handwashing, mask-wearing, and social distancing.

Friendly Greetings: Greet clients warmly and with a friendly smile as they enter your barbershop. A welcoming first impression sets the tone for their experience.

Comfortable Waiting Area: Provide a comfortable and clean waiting area for clients. Offer seating, reading materials, and refreshments to make their wait enjoyable.

Personalized Service: Engage in personalized consultations with clients to understand their preferences and desired outcomes. Tailor your services accordingly.

Listen to Clients: Actively listen to your clients during consultations and throughout the grooming process. Show genuine interest in their needs and concerns.

Expert Advice: Offer professional advice and recommendations based on your expertise. Suggest suitable hairstyles or beard designs that complement your clients' features.

Explain the Process: Communicate the steps of the grooming service to your clients so they know what to expect and feel comfortable during the process.

Respect Client Privacy: Respect client privacy and avoid sharing personal information about them with others.

Provide Clean Capes and Neck Strips: Use fresh and clean capes and neck strips for each client to maintain hygiene and prevent cross-contamination.

Professional Appearance: Present yourself in a professional and well-groomed manner. Your appearance reflects the overall atmosphere of your barbershop.

Create a Relaxing Environment: Play soothing music or provide calming scents to create a relaxed and enjoyable atmosphere.

Offer Refreshments: Provide complimentary refreshments like water, coffee, or tea to make clients feel pampered.

Follow-Up: After the service, follow up with clients to ensure they are satisfied with their haircut or grooming. Send thank-you messages or ask for feedback to show you care about their experience.

By consistently implementing these practices, you can create a safe and welcoming environment that leaves a positive impression on your clients. A comfortable and enjoyable atmosphere encourages clients to return for future services and refer others to your barbershop, ultimately contributing to your business's success and growth.

CHAPTER 9: PERSONAL BRANDING AND PROFESSIONAL IMAGE

9a. Developing Your Unique Brand As A Barber

Leveraging personal branding can significantly contribute to your business success as a barber. Personal branding is about showcasing your unique identity, expertise, and values to attract clients and build a loyal following. Here are some ways to utilize personal branding effectively:

Define Your Brand Identity: Identify your unique strengths, skills, and the value you bring as a barber. Understand your target audience and what sets you apart from other barbers in the area.

Create a Professional Image: Invest in professional attire and a well-groomed appearance that aligns with your brand identity. Your personal presentation is part of your branding.

Establish an Online Presence: Build a strong online presence through social media platforms, a professional website, and relevant online directories. Showcase your work, share grooming tips, and engage with your audience.

Share Your Story: Share your journey, experiences, and passion for barbering with your clients. A compelling personal story can forge a deeper connection with your audience.

Consistent Branding Elements: Use consistent branding elements, such as a logo, color scheme, and tone of voice, across all your marketing materials and social media platforms.

Highlight Your Expertise: Position yourself as an expert in your field by sharing grooming tutorials, before-and-after transformations, and grooming advice.

Engage with Your Audience: Respond to comments, messages, and inquiries promptly. Engaging with your audience builds a sense of community and strengthens your brand.

Use Video Content: Utilize video content to showcase your skills, demonstrate grooming techniques, and share behind-the-scenes glimpses of your barbershop.

Collaborate with Influencers: Partner with local influencers or social media personalities to reach a broader audience and gain exposure for your barbering business.

Host Events or Workshops: Organize grooming workshops, themed events, or barbering demonstrations to showcase your expertise and attract new clients.

Obtain Client Testimonials: Encourage satisfied clients to provide testimonials that highlight their positive experiences with your services. Share these testimonials on your website and social media.

Be Authentic and Genuine: Stay true to your brand values and personality. Authenticity builds trust with your audience and clients.

Network and Collaborate: Collaborate with other local businesses or professionals in related industries to cross-promote services and expand your network.

By strategically leveraging personal branding, you can establish yourself as a reputable and sought-after barber, attract a loyal clientele, and differentiate yourself in a competitive market. Your personal brand becomes a powerful tool for building your business and achieving long-term success as a barber.

9b. Dressing The Part And Maintaining A Professional Appearance

Dressing the part and maintaining a professional appearance are crucial aspects of being a successful barber. Here's why they are essential:

Client Perception: Your appearance creates the first impression on your clients. Dressing professionally instills confidence and trust in your clients, making them feel they are in capable hands.

Brand Image: Your appearance is a reflection of your personal brand as a barber. It communicates your style, professionalism, and attention to detail, contributing to your overall brand image.

Client Comfort: Clients are more likely to feel at ease and comfortable with a well-groomed and well-dressed barber. This relaxed atmosphere enhances the overall client experience.

Building Trust: A professional appearance builds trust with your clients. It signals that you take your role seriously and are committed to providing high-quality services.

Setting Expectations: Your appearance sets the tone for the barbershop's atmosphere and level of professionalism. Clients will have certain expectations based on your appearance, and you want to meet or exceed those expectations.

Confidence and Respect: Dressing professionally boosts your confidence, which positively impacts your interactions with clients. It also shows respect for your profession and your clients.

Inspiring Client Loyalty: Clients are more likely to return to a barber who maintains a consistent and professional appearance. Building loyal clientele is essential for business success.

Role Modeling: As a barber, you serve as a role model for grooming and style. A professional appearance sets an example for clients to follow, reinforcing the importance of personal care.

Competitive Advantage: In a competitive industry, a professional appearance can be a differentiating factor that attracts clients to choose your services over others.

Barbershop Reputation: Your appearance contributes to the overall reputation of your barbershop. A team of well-dressed and professional barbers enhances the barbershop's image.

Self-Expression: Dressing the part allows you to express your personal style and identity as a barber. It can help you build a unique brand and stand out in the industry.

Safety and Hygiene: A professional appearance goes hand in hand with maintaining hygiene standards. Clean and well-groomed barbers help ensure a safe and hygienic environment for clients.

In summary, dressing the part and maintaining a professional appearance are integral to building a positive image as a barber. A professional presentation enhances client perception, trust, and loyalty, while also contributing to the overall success and reputation of your barbershop.

9c. Leveraging Personal Branding For Business Success

Leveraging personal branding can significantly contribute to your business success by helping you stand out in a competitive market, building a loyal clientele, and establishing yourself as a reputable expert in your industry. Here's how you can use personal branding to achieve business success:

Define Your Unique Identity: Identify your strengths, values, and passions as a professional. Understanding what makes you unique will be the foundation of your personal brand.

Identify Your Target Audience: Determine your ideal clients and understand their needs and preferences. Tailor your brand messaging and services to appeal directly to your target audience.

Create a Professional Online Presence: Build a strong online presence through a professional website, active social media profiles, and relevant industry platforms. Showcase your expertise, share valuable content, and engage with your audience.

Consistency in Branding: Maintain consistency in your branding elements, such as your logo, color scheme, and brand voice. This coherence reinforces your identity and helps clients recognize your brand easily.

Share Your Story: Communicate your journey, experiences, and passion for your field. Your personal story humanizes your brand and builds connections with your audience.

Highlight Your Expertise: Demonstrate your knowledge and skills by sharing educational content, industry insights, and success stories related to your business.

Engage with Your Audience: Interact with your audience regularly. Respond to comments, messages, and inquiries promptly to show your commitment to customer service.

Offer Value Through Content: Share valuable content that addresses your audience's pain points and provides solutions to their problems. This positions you as a helpful resource and expert in your field.

Build a Network and Collaborate: Establish relationships with other professionals and influencers in your industry. Collaborating with like-minded individuals can expand your reach and credibility.

Consistently Deliver on Your Promise: Your personal brand should align with the quality of service you provide. Consistently deliver exceptional experiences to build a positive reputation and gain referrals.

Seek Testimonials and Reviews: Encourage satisfied clients to provide testimonials and reviews. Positive feedback reinforces the trustworthiness of your brand.

Continuously Learn and Grow: Stay updated with industry trends, technologies, and best practices. Continuous learning demonstrates your commitment to excellence.

Monitor and Measure Your Brand Success: Regularly assess the impact of your personal branding efforts. Use analytics to track website traffic, social media engagement, and business growth.

Be Authentic and Transparent: Be true to yourself and your values. Authenticity fosters trust and creates meaningful connections with your audience.

By strategically leveraging personal branding, you can position yourself as a standout professional, attract a loyal client base, and gain a competitive advantage in your industry. Your personal brand becomes a powerful tool for achieving business success and fostering long-term growth.

* * *

CHAPTER 10: NAVIGATING LEGAL AND LICENSING REQUIREMENTS

10a. Understanding Local Regulations And Licensing

Understanding local regulations and licensing requirements is crucial for operating a legal and compliant barbershop. Here's the best way to go about it:

Research Government Websites: Start by visiting the official websites of your local government and relevant regulatory agencies. Look for information on barbering regulations, licensing, and health and safety guidelines.

Contact Local Licensing Authorities: Reach out to your city or county's licensing department or health department. They can provide detailed information about the specific licenses and permits required for barbers in your area.

Attend Workshops or Seminars: Look for workshops or seminars organized by local business associations or barbering organizations. These events often cover regulatory compliance and licensing information.

Consult with Experienced Barbers: Speak with experienced barbers in your community who are familiar with local regulations. They may provide insights and guidance based on their own experiences.

Join Professional Associations: Consider joining professional barbering associations in your country or region. These organizations often provide resources and updates on industry regulations.

Read Barbering Industry Publications: Stay informed about industry regulations by reading barbering magazines, online publications, and blogs that cover legal and licensing topics.

Engage with Legal Professionals: Consult with legal professionals who specialize in business and licensing matters. They can provide tailored advice based on your specific location and situation.

Check Zoning Requirements: Ensure that your barbershop location complies with local zoning regulations. Some areas may have specific zoning restrictions for commercial properties.

Stay Updated: Be proactive in staying up-to-date with any changes or updates to local regulations that may affect your barbershop business.

Review Health and Safety Guidelines: Understand the health and safety guidelines specific to barbering services, especially those related to sanitation and sterilization.

Get Licensed and Certified: Complete any required training or educational programs necessary for obtaining your barbering license. Some areas may also require additional certifications for certain services.

Adhere to Environmental Regulations: Comply with environmental regulations, such as waste disposal and chemical handling guidelines, to maintain a safe and eco-friendly barbershop.

10b. Insurance Considerations For Barbers

Insurance is an essential aspect of protecting your barbershop business and managing potential risks. Here are some insurance considerations for barbers:

General Liability Insurance: This type of insurance provides coverage for bodily injury, property damage, and personal injury claims that may arise from accidents at your barbershop. It protects you from legal and financial liabilities.

Professional Liability Insurance: Also known as Errors and Omissions (E&O) insurance, professional liability insurance covers claims of negligence, errors, or omissions in your services. It is particularly important for barbers to safeguard against claims related to unsatisfactory haircuts or grooming services.

Business Property Insurance: This insurance protects your barbershop's physical assets, including equipment, furniture, and inventory, in case of theft, fire, or other covered perils.

Business Interruption Insurance: Business interruption insurance provides coverage for lost income and ongoing expenses if your barbershop faces a temporary closure due to a covered event, such as a fire or natural disaster.

Workers' Compensation Insurance: If you have employees, workers' compensation insurance is often mandatory. It covers medical expenses and lost wages for employees who are injured or become ill while on the job.

Commercial Auto Insurance: If you use a vehicle for business purposes, such as transporting equipment or making house calls, commercial auto insurance is necessary to protect against accidents and liabilities.

Cyber Liability Insurance: If your barbershop stores sensitive client information digitally, cyber liability insurance can help cover the costs associated with data breaches or cyber-attacks.

Employment Practices Liability Insurance (EPLI): EPLI provides coverage against claims related to employment-related issues, such as discrimination, harassment, or wrongful termination, brought by current or former employees.

Product Liability Insurance: If you sell grooming products or other items at your barbershop, product liability insurance can protect you from claims related to product defects or injuries caused by the products.

Business Owner's Policy (BOP): A BOP bundles general liability, property insurance, and often includes business interruption coverage. It's a cost-effective way for small businesses, including barbershops, to get essential coverage.

Renters Insurance: If you rent the space for your barbershop, consider renters insurance to protect your belongings and equipment within the rented property.

Fidelity Bond/Crime Insurance: This type of insurance can protect your barbershop from financial losses due to employee theft, fraud, or dishonesty.

It's crucial to assess your barbershop's specific needs and risks to determine the appropriate insurance coverage. Working with an experienced insurance agent or broker who understands the unique requirements of the barbering industry can help you tailor a comprehensive insurance policy that adequately protects your business and assets.

10c. Protecting Your Business And Assets

Protecting your business and assets as a barber involves implementing various strategies to mitigate risks and ensure the longevity of your barbershop. Here are some key steps to consider:

Obtain Insurance Coverage: Invest in appropriate insurance policies, such as general liability insurance, professional liability insurance, property insurance, workers' compensation insurance (if you have employees), and any other relevant coverage specific to your business needs.

Incorporate or Form an LLC: Consider forming a legal entity for your barbershop, such as a Limited Liability Company (LLC) or corporation. This can provide personal liability protection for your personal assets in case of legal claims against your business.

Create and Follow Contracts: Develop clear and comprehensive client service contracts that outline your terms of service, cancellation policies, and any other relevant agreements. Contracts can help protect your business in case of disputes or misunderstandings.

Practice Good Hygiene and Safety: Adhere to strict hygiene and safety protocols to protect your clients, employees, and yourself from potential risks or accidents.

Train and Educate Employees: If you have employees, ensure they receive proper training on safety, customer service, and industry best practices. Well-trained staff can help prevent accidents and provide high-quality services.

Secure Your Digital Data: Protect client information and business data by implementing strong cybersecurity measures and using secure systems for data storage.

Implement Financial Controls: Establish financial controls and separate business and personal finances. Regularly monitor your barbershop's financial health and expenses.

Maintain Proper Licensing and Permits: Ensure your barbershop is compliant with all local regulations, licensing requirements, and health and safety permits.

Regularly Inspect Equipment: Regularly inspect and maintain your barbering equipment to ensure it is in good working condition and safe to use.

Have an Emergency Plan: Create a contingency plan for emergencies, such as natural disasters or unexpected closures, to minimize potential disruptions to your business.

Secure Your Premises: Take necessary security measures to protect your barbershop from theft or vandalism. Consider installing security cameras and alarm systems.

Backup Important Documents: Keep digital and physical copies of important business documents, such as licenses, insurance policies, and financial records, in secure locations.

Stay Compliant with Tax Obligations: Comply with all tax requirements, including filing accurate tax returns and paying taxes on time.

Seek Legal and Financial Advice: Consult with professionals, such as attorneys and accountants, who specialize in small businesses and the barbering industry. They can provide valuable guidance and advice tailored to your specific needs.

By taking these proactive measures, you can safeguard your barbershop business and assets, minimize potential risks, and focus on providing exceptional services to your clients with peace of mind.

* * *

CHAPTER 11: MANAGING FINANCES AND PRICING STRATEGIES

11a. Budgeting And Financial Planning For Barbers

As a barber, budgeting and financial planning are essential for managing your business's finances effectively and achieving long-term financial stability. Here are some key considerations:

Start-up Costs: Calculate the initial costs required to set up your barbershop, including rent, equipment, furniture, licenses, insurance, and marketing materials.

Operating Expenses: Identify and estimate your monthly operating expenses, such as rent, utilities, inventory, marketing, payroll (if you have employees), and other recurring costs.

Pricing Strategy: Set appropriate prices for your services to cover your expenses while remaining competitive in the market. Consider your target audience, location, and the value you offer.

Revenue Projections: Create revenue projections based on your expected number of clients, average service prices, and the frequency of visits. This will help you set financial goals for your business.

Emergency Fund: Set aside an emergency fund to cover unexpected expenses or fluctuations in revenue. Having a financial buffer can help you navigate challenging times.

Debt Management: If you have loans or debts, create a plan to manage them effectively. Consider paying off high-interest debts first to reduce financial burdens.

Savings and Investments: Develop a savings plan and consider investment opportunities to grow your personal wealth and secure your financial future.

Tax Planning: Stay organized with your financial records and engage with a tax professional to ensure compliance with tax regulations and maximize deductions.

Bookkeeping and Accounting: Maintain accurate financial records and consider using accounting software to track income, expenses, and profits effectively.

Review Financial Performance: Regularly review your financial statements, analyze trends, and identify areas for improvement or cost-saving measures.

Set Financial Goals: Define short-term and long-term financial goals for your barbershop. Establish specific, measurable, achievable, relevant, and time-bound (SMART) objectives.

Cost Control: Continuously look for ways to reduce costs without compromising the quality of your services. Negotiate better deals with suppliers and explore cost-effective marketing strategies.

Cash Flow Management: Monitor your cash flow to ensure you have enough liquidity to cover expenses and investments.

Plan for Retirement: Develop a retirement plan and consider contributing to retirement accounts to secure your financial future beyond your barbering career.

Having a well-thought-out budgeting and financial planning strategy can help you make informed decisions, weather financial challenges, and position your barbershop for sustainable growth and success. If you are unsure about financial matters, consider seeking advice from a financial advisor or an accountant with experience in small businesses and the barbering industry.

11b. Pricing Your Services Competitively And Fairly

Pricing your services competitively and fairly as a barber involves finding a balance that reflects the value you provide while remaining competitive in the market. Here's the best approach to determine your pricing:

Research Competitors: Start by researching other barbershops in your local area to understand their pricing structure. Analyze what services they offer and at what price points.

Consider Your Experience and Expertise: Your level of experience and expertise should be reflected in your pricing. If you have specialized skills or certifications, it may justify higher rates.

Calculate Costs: Determine your operating expenses, including rent, utilities, insurance, equipment, and product costs. Consider how much revenue you need to cover these expenses and make a profit.

Value Proposition: Define your unique selling points and the value you offer to your clients. Consider factors such as exceptional customer service, personalized consultations, and the overall experience you provide.

Client Demographics: Understand your target audience and their willingness to pay for your services. Pricing should align with what your ideal clients perceive as a fair value.

Service Differentiation: Differentiate your services based on the level of service, quality of products, or additional perks you offer. Adjust pricing accordingly for premium or specialized services.

Tiered Pricing: Consider implementing tiered pricing based on the complexity of the service or the time required. This allows clients to choose the level of service that fits their budget and needs.

Seasonal Promotions: Offer seasonal promotions or discounts to attract new clients or incentivize existing ones to try new services.

Test and Adjust: Start with a competitive price point and monitor how clients respond. If necessary, be willing to adjust your pricing based on client feedback and market demand.

Maintain Consistency: Be consistent with your pricing and avoid frequent changes, as it may create confusion for clients and undermine your brand's credibility.

Package Deals: Consider offering package deals or loyalty programs to encourage repeat business and build customer loyalty.

Communicate Value: Clearly communicate the value of your services to clients. Explain the benefits they will receive from choosing your barbershop over others.

Track Profitability: Regularly review your financial reports to assess the profitability of your services. Identify which services are the most profitable and focus on promoting them.

Continuously Improve: Keep an eye on industry trends, client preferences, and changes in the market. Continuously improve your skills and services to justify your pricing.

By taking these factors into account and striking a balance between competitive pricing and the value you provide, you can position your barbershop for success in the market while maintaining fairness to both your clients and your business.

11c. Tracking Expenses And Maximizing Profitability

Tracking expenses and maximizing profitability as a barber requires effective financial management and record-keeping. Here's the best way to achieve this:

Maintain Accurate Records: Keep detailed records of all your business expenses, including rent, utilities, supplies, equipment, marketing, insurance, and any other costs related to running your barbershop.

Use Accounting Software: Consider using accounting software to track income, expenses, and profits. Accounting tools can simplify financial management and generate reports to assess your business's financial health.

Categorize Expenses: Organize your expenses into categories to easily identify where your money is going. Common expense categories for barbershops include rent, utilities, equipment, supplies, and marketing.

Separate Business and Personal Finances: Keep your personal and business finances separate. Have dedicated bank accounts and credit cards for your barbershop to avoid confusion and make expense tracking more manageable.

Set Budgets: Create a budget for your barbershop, setting limits for each expense category. Regularly review your actual expenses against the budget to identify areas where you can cut costs.

Negotiate with Suppliers: Negotiate better deals with suppliers to get discounts on products and supplies, which can help reduce your expenses.

Monitor Profit Margins: Calculate the profit margin for each service you offer. Focus on promoting and offering services with higher profit margins to increase your overall profitability.

Price Services Appropriately: Ensure your service prices cover both direct costs (e.g., products used) and indirect costs (e.g., rent, utilities). Don't underprice your services, as it can impact profitability.

Analyze Profitability Reports: Regularly review financial reports to assess your barbershop's profitability. Identify which services generate the most revenue and which ones might need adjustments.

Cut Unnecessary Costs: Identify and eliminate unnecessary expenses that don't contribute significantly to your business's success.

Offer Value-Added Services: Consider offering additional services or packages that can increase the perceived value for clients and boost profitability.

Promote High-Margin Services: Promote services with higher profit margins through marketing efforts and incentives.

Evaluate Employee Productivity: If you have employees, assess their productivity and ensure their contributions are positively impacting your barbershop's profitability.

Stay Informed: Stay informed about industry trends, pricing strategies, and changes in the market to make informed decisions that can optimize profitability.

By diligently tracking expenses, analyzing profitability, and making strategic financial decisions, you can maximize the profitability of your barbershop business while maintaining a strong financial foundation. Regularly review your financial performance and make adjustments as needed to achieve long-term success.

* * *

CHAPTER 12: THRIVING IN THE BARBERING INDUSTRY

12a. Embracing Innovation And Staying Up-To-Date With Trends

Embracing innovation and staying up-to-date with trends is crucial in the ever-evolving field of barbering. Here are some effective ways to stay current and innovative in your barbering practice:

Attend Workshops and Seminars: Participate in barbering workshops, seminars, and industry events. These gatherings provide opportunities to learn from experts, discover new techniques, and stay updated with emerging trends.

Join Professional Associations: Become a member of barbering associations or organizations. They often offer access to educational resources, networking opportunities, and updates on industry advancements.

Follow Industry Influencers: Follow influential barbers and grooming experts on social media platforms. Engaging with their content can keep you informed about the latest trends and techniques.

Subscribe to Barbering Magazines and Blogs: Read barbering magazines and online blogs to gain insights into industry trends, product reviews, and expert advice.

Participate in Online Forums: Join online barbering forums or communities where professionals share knowledge, experiences, and trends.

Continuous Learning: Commit to continuous learning and professional development. Enroll in courses or certifications to enhance your skills and knowledge.

Experiment and Practice: Be open to experimenting with new techniques and styles. Practicing on models or mannequins allows you to refine your skills and explore creative expression.

Encourage Client Feedback: Encourage honest feedback from clients about their preferences and expectations. It helps you understand evolving client demands.

Stay Updated with Grooming Products: Keep yourself informed about the latest grooming products, tools, and equipment in the market. Stay open to incorporating innovative products into your services.

Follow Fashion and Pop Culture: Stay aware of fashion trends, popular culture, and celebrity grooming styles. These influences often shape client preferences.

Collaborate with Peers: Collaborate with other barbers or professionals in the grooming industry. Sharing insights and experiences can lead to innovative ideas and practices.

Participate in Competitions: Consider participating in barbering competitions to challenge yourself and gain exposure to cutting-edge styles and techniques.

Offer Specialized Services: Consider adding specialized services like beard grooming, facial hair design, or hair tattooing to cater to diverse client demands.

Use Social Media for Inspiration: Utilize social media platforms like Instagram and Pinterest to discover and share new trends, styles, and inspiration with your clients.

By actively seeking out new knowledge, embracing creativity, and being receptive to change, you can maintain a cutting-edge barbering practice and provide your clients with innovative and on-trend grooming experiences.

12b. Balancing Work-Life And Self-Care As A Barber

Balancing work, life, and self-care as a barber is essential for maintaining overall well-being and ensuring long-term success in your career. Here are some effective ways to achieve this balance:

Set Boundaries: Establish clear boundaries between work and personal life. Determine specific working hours and stick to them to create a work-life balance.

Schedule Time Off: Plan regular breaks and time off to recharge and spend quality time with family and friends.

Delegate Tasks: If you have employees or assistants, delegate tasks to free up some of your time and reduce workload stress.

Prioritize Self-Care: Make self-care a priority. Set aside time for activities that rejuvenate you, such as exercise, hobbies, or meditation.

Manage Workload: Avoid overbooking or taking on more clients than you can handle comfortably. Prioritize quality over quantity.

Plan Personal Time: Schedule personal activities and commitments on your calendar to ensure they are given equal importance to work-related tasks.

Use Technology Wisely: Utilize scheduling tools, apps, or software to streamline your business operations and manage appointments efficiently.

Ask for Help: Don't hesitate to seek support from family, friends, or colleagues when needed. Share responsibilities when possible.

Communicate with Clients: Keep clients informed of your availability and any changes in your schedule to manage their expectations.

Create a Relaxing Workspace: Make your barbershop environment pleasant and relaxing to reduce stress for both you and your clients.

Take Short Breaks: Incorporate short breaks between appointments to recharge and prepare for the next client.

Learn Time Management: Develop effective time management skills to maximize productivity during working hours and create more time for personal life.

Regular Exercise: Engage in regular physical activity to reduce stress and improve overall well-being.

Practice Mindfulness: Incorporate mindfulness practices into your daily routine to stay present and reduce anxiety.

Achieving work-life balance and self-care as a barber requires intentional planning and prioritization. Here are some specific strategies to help you maintain this balance:

Set Clear Working Hours: Establish specific working hours and communicate them to your clients. Stick to these hours to create a clear boundary between work and personal life.

Limit Appointments: Avoid overbooking or taking on more clients than you can comfortably manage. Allow time between appointments for breaks and personal activities.

Schedule Self-Care Time: Block out time in your schedule for self-care activities, such as exercise, hobbies, meditation, or spending time with loved ones.

Delegate Tasks: If you have employees or assistants, delegate non-client-related tasks to free up time for yourself.

Take Regular Breaks: Incorporate short breaks throughout your workday to rest, recharge, and refocus.

Use Technology to Streamline: Utilize scheduling apps or software to manage appointments efficiently and reduce administrative burdens.

Prioritize Health and Nutrition: Pay attention to your physical health by maintaining a balanced diet, staying hydrated, and getting enough rest.

Practice Stress Management: Adopt stress-relief techniques like deep breathing, mindfulness, or yoga to manage work-related stress.

Communicate Boundaries: Make sure your clients and colleagues are aware of your boundaries and respect your personal time.

Create a Relaxing Workspace: Design your barbershop environment to be a calming and enjoyable space for both you and your clients.

Regularly Review Your Schedule: Assess your schedule regularly to identify areas where you can make improvements to achieve better balance.

Learn to Say No: Be mindful of taking on additional commitments that may disrupt your work-life balance. Learn to say no when necessary.

Limit Screen Time: Reduce excessive screen time outside of work to prioritize real-life interactions and relaxation.

Make Time for Hobbies: Engage in hobbies and activities you enjoy to recharge and boost creativity.

Remember that work-life balance and self-care are individual pursuits, and what works for one person may not work for another. Customize these strategies to fit your unique needs and preferences. By consistently prioritizing self-care and setting boundaries, you can maintain a healthier work-life balance as a barber and lead a fulfilling life both inside and outside of your barbershop.

12c. Contributions To The Community And Giving Back

As a barber, there are several meaningful ways you can give back to your community and make valuable contributions. Here are some ideas:

Offer Free or Discounted Services: Organize community events where you provide free or discounted haircuts to those in need, such as the homeless, low-income individuals, or students.

Partner with Local Charities: Collaborate with local charities or non-profit organizations to offer your services at their events or fundraising initiatives.

Support Community Events: Participate in local community events, fairs, or school programs, offering your barbering services as part of the festivities.

Mentorship Programs: Volunteer to mentor aspiring barbers or young individuals interested in pursuing a career in the industry. Share your knowledge and experience to inspire the next generation.

Participate in Back-to-School Drives: Contribute to back-to-school drives by providing free haircuts to students in preparation for the new academic year.

Senior Care Facilities: Visit senior care homes or facilities and offer grooming services to residents who may have mobility challenges or limited access to barbershops.

Emergency Response Support: Offer your services to support emergency responders, such as firefighters or medical personnel, during community events or special occasions.

Career Days at Schools: Participate in career days at local schools, where you can talk about your profession and offer grooming demonstrations.

Barbershop Fundraisers: Host fundraisers at your barbershop for charitable causes or local community projects. Donate a portion of the proceeds to the selected charity.

Support Local Sports Teams: Sponsor local sports teams or community events to show your support and involvement in the neighborhood.

Hair Donation Drives: Organize hair donation drives, where clients can choose to have their hair cut and donated to organizations that make wigs for people with medical hair loss conditions.

Educational Workshops: Offer educational workshops on grooming and personal care for community members to enhance their self-confidence and self-esteem.

Veteran Support: Partner with veterans' organizations to provide grooming services to veterans and active-duty military personnel.

Environmental Initiatives: Adopt eco-friendly practices in your barbershop to contribute to environmental sustainability and promote eco-consciousness in your community.

When giving back to your community, it's essential to identify causes and initiatives that align with your values and passions. Your contributions as a barber can have a positive impact on the lives of others and foster a strong sense of community within your area.

Ready, Set, Let's Go!

- If you have not already, create an account with one of the appointment platforms. We recommend The Cut (www.thecut.co). The Pro Subscription is $20 per month but they also have a free trial period and a lite option which is free. We recognize that every dollar counts but this app pretty much pays for itself and it's also is a step toward presenting yourself as a professional.

In the about section of your app, ask your clients to please be prompt and specify that you have "no-wait appointments." This informs the client right away that you're respectful of their time. Depending on your speed, you can book every 1/2 hour or one client per hour. Also, be certain to create a statement when clients book such as "Thanks for booking" or "Your booking is confirmed."

- Next, create your social media pages i.e. Instagram, Tiktok, etc. Be sure to present your best work. If you have not had success with your current pages you want to consider rebranding. That may involve creating your niche in your market such as a name change or building a reputation for certain haircut or promotion. Which leads us to the next step.

- As a barber, running call-to-action promotions can be an effective way to attract new customers to your barbershop. Here are some creative and enticing promotions you can consider:

Early Bird Special: This could be a discount for clients that are early risers and would be looking to save a few bucks. Think of this as killing two birds with one stone. You'd be increasing your revenue, attracting the more frugal clients, and building business on those days that you may not be the busiest.

First-Time Customer Discount: Offer a special discount or percentage off the first haircut for new customers.

Refer-a-Friend Program: Implement a referral program where both the existing customer and the referred friend receive a discount on their next visit.

Seasonal Promotions: Create limited-time seasonal promotions, such as "Back to School Specials," "Holiday Grooming Packages," or "Summer Refresh Deals."

Bundle Services: Package services together at a discounted rate, like "Haircut and Beard Trim Combo" or "Grooming Package for Special Occasions."

Social Media Exclusive Offers: Encourage people to follow your social media accounts by offering exclusive discounts or promotions to your online followers.

Flash Sales: Run spontaneous flash sales for a few hours or a day, offering discounted services during that period.

Loyalty Program: Implement a loyalty program where customers earn points for each visit and can redeem them for free or discounted services.

Student and Senior Discounts: Offer special discounts for students and seniors to cater to different age groups in your community.

Community Event Sponsorship: Sponsor a local community event or sports team and provide exclusive discounts to attendees or team members.

Free Add-On Service: Provide a complimentary add-on service, such as a hot towel treatment or a scalp massage, with any regular haircut.

Membership Subscription: Offer a membership subscription that includes a fixed number of haircuts per month at a reduced price.

Social Media Contests: Run contests on social media with hair-related themes, and offer a free haircut or grooming package as the prize.

Punch Cards: Create punch cards that reward customers with a free service after a certain number of visits.

Charity Events: Host charity events or donation drives where a portion of the proceeds goes to a local charity, giving customers an opportunity to support a good cause.

When running promotions, make sure to communicate them effectively through your barbershop's website, social media channels, and in-store signage. Create eye-catching visuals and use compelling language to entice potential customers. Remember to set clear start and end dates for the promotions to create a sense of urgency. By offering attractive promotions and providing excellent service, you can encourage new customers to try your barbershop and turn them into loyal clients.

Last but not least, if you're ever in need of t-shirts for your business, scan the QR code below and get a 10% discount on every purchase. Simply apply the code BOOK at checkout.

Best of Luck In Your Cutting Endeavors,

Dack Douglas

www.ingramcontent.com/pod-product-compliance
Lightning Source LLC
Chambersburg PA
CBHW060609120726
48002CB00010B/2895